ROUND AND ROUND THE GARDEN

Compiled by Sarah Williams
Illustrated by Ian Beck

Oxford University Press

Oxford University Press, Walton Street, Oxford OX2 6DP

Oxford New York Toronto
Delhi Bombay Calcutta Madras Karachi
Petaling Jaya Singapore Hong Kong Tokyo
Nairobi Dar es Salaam Cape Town
Melbourne Auckland

and associated companies in
Berlin Ibadan

Oxford is a trade mark of Oxford University Press

Selection, arrangement and editorial matter
© Oxford University Press 1983
First published 1983
First printed in paperback 1984
Reprinted 1984, 1985 (thrice), 1986, 1987 (twice), 1988 (twice), 1989

Williams, Sarah
Round and round the garden.
1. Finger play.
I. Title
398'.8 GV1218.F5
ISBN 0-19-272132-1

Phototypeset by Tradespools Ltd, Frome, Somerset
Printed in Hong Kong

for Beth, Daniel, Edmund, Eleanor
Jacqueline, Richard, Samantha and Thomas.

Contents

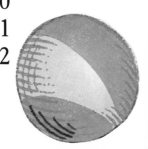

Round and round the garden

Round and round the garden
Like a teddy bear;
One step, two step,
Tickle you under there!

Circle child's palm with finger.

Round and round the garden . . .

Walk finger slowly up arm.

. . . one step . . . two step . . .

Tickle child suddenly under arm.

. . . Tickle you under there!

Five fat sausages

Five fat sausages frying in a pan,
All of a sudden one went 'BANG!'

Four fat sausages, *etc.*
Three fat sausages, *etc.*
Two fat sausages, *etc.*
One fat sausage frying in a pan,
All of a sudden it went 'Bang!'
and there were NO sausages left!

Hold up five fingers.   Clap hands loudly.   Hold up four fingers.   Clap hands again.   Continue until no fingers (sausages) left.

Five fat sausages . . .   All of a sudden one went BANG!   Four fat sausages . . .   NO sausages . . .

Foxy's hole

Put your finger in Foxy's hole.
Foxy's not at home.
Foxy's out at the back door
A-picking at a bone.

Interlock fingers making hole between middle and ring finger.

Get child to put finger in hole.

Nip child's finger lightly with thumbs.

Put your finger in foxy's hole.

Foxy's not at home.

A-picking at a bone.

9

Clap, clap hands

Clap, clap hands, one, two, three,
Put your hands upon your knees,
Lift them high to touch the sky,
Clap, clap hands and away they fly.

Perform actions in rhythm.

Clap, clap hands, one, two, three,

. . . your knees.

Lift them high . . . to touch the sky,

Clap, clap hands and away they fly.

The apple tree

Here is the tree with leaves so green.

Here are the apples that hang between.

When the wind blows the apples fall.

Here is a basket to gather them all.

Make tree with arms.

Here is the tree . . .

Clench fists.

Here are the apples . . .

Wave arms as if in wind and let fists fall suddenly.

. . . the apples fall

Make a basket with both hands.

Here is the basket to gather them all.

11

Piggy on the railway

Piggy on the railway,
Picking up stones;
Along came an engine
And broke Piggy's bones.

'Oh!' said Piggy,
'That's not fair.'
'Oh!' said the engine driver,
'I don't care!'

Mime picking up stones.

Bang fists against palm.

Raise hands in surprise and anger.

Shrug shoulders and turn away.

Piggy on the railway,
picking up stones.

Along came an engine,
and BROKE piggy's bones.

'Oh!' said Piggy,
'That's not fair.'

'Oh!' said the engine driver,
'I don't care!'

The Ostrich

Here is the ostrich straight and tall,
Nodding his head above us all.
Here is the hedgehog prickly and small,
Rolling himself into a ball.
Here is the spider scuttling around,
Treading so lightly on the ground.
Here are the birds that fly so high,
Spreading their wings across the sky.
Here are the children fast asleep,
And in the night the owls do peep,
Tuit tuwhoo, tuit tuwhoo.

Raise arm for ostrich.

Here is the ostrich...

Hold fingers as in panel then close up into a ball.

Here is the hedgehog . . .

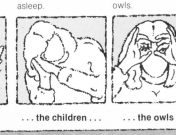

Turn hand over for spider.

Here is the spider...

Interlock hands for bird.

. . .the birds . . .

Pretend to be asleep.

. . . the children . . .

Ring eyes for owls.

. . . the owls . . .

My house

I'm going to build a little house
   with a chimney tall,
A sloping roof—and a garden wall,
A big front door you can open wide,
And two tiny windows you can peep inside.
I'm going to build a table big enough for two,
Two little chairs—one for me—one for you.
Knock at the knocker, and please come in
My little house is shining like a bright new pin.

Raise arm for chimney.

Hands draw roof and wall.

Open hands for door.

Ring eyes for windows.

Point to self and child for chairs, and pretend to knock on a door. Finally open hands wide to welcome guests.

chimney tall,

A sloping roof and a garden wall,

A big front door you can open wide,

And two tiny windows you can peep inside,

My little house is shining like a bright new pin.

Mousie

Mousie comes a-creeping, creeping.
Mousie comes a-peeping, peeping.
Mousie said, 'I'd like to stay,
But I haven't time today.'
Mousie popped into his hole
And said, 'Achoo!
I've caught a cold!'

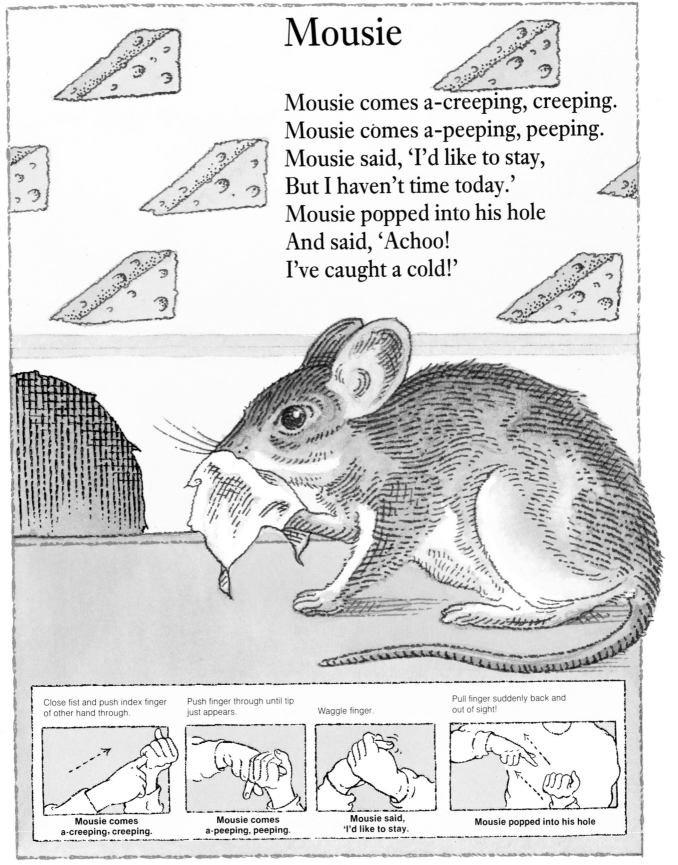

Close fist and push index finger of other hand through.

Push finger through until tip just appears.

Waggle finger.

Pull finger suddenly back and out of sight!

Mousie comes a-creeping, creeping.

Mousie comes a-peeping, peeping.

Mousie said, 'I'd like to stay.

Mousie popped into his hole

Ten little men

Ten little men standing straight,
Ten little men open the gate,
Ten little men all in a ring,
Ten little men bow to the king,
Ten little men dance all day,
Ten little men hide away.

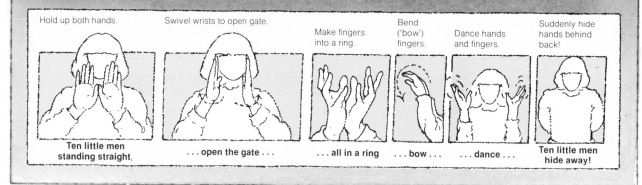

Hold up both hands.

Swivel wrists to open gate.

Make fingers into a ring.

Bend ('bow') fingers.

Dance hands and fingers.

Suddenly hide hands behind back!

Ten little men standing straight,

. . . open the gate . . .

. . . all in a ring

. . . bow . . .

. . . dance . . .

Ten little men hide away!

Incy, wincy spider

Incy, wincy spider
Climbing up the spout.
Down came the rain
And washed the spider out.

Out came the sun
And dried up all the rain,
So incy wincy spider
Climbed up the spout again.

Opposite thumb and index fingers climb up
each other. alternately.

Incy, wincy spider
Climbing up the spout

Show rain falling

Down came the rain

make
a large
circle.

Out came the sun

Opposite thumbs and forefingers Climb
up each other again.

Climbed up the spout again.

17

Ten little fingers

I have ten little fingers,
And they all belong to me.
I can make them do things,
Would you like to see?
I can shut them up tight,
Or open them all wide.

Put them all together,
Or make them all hide.
I can make them jump high;
I can make them jump low.
I can fold them quietly,
And hold them all just so.

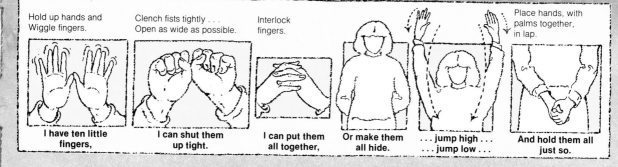

Hold up hands and
Wiggle fingers.

Clench fists tightly . . .
Open as wide as possible.

Interlock
fingers.

Place hands, with
palms together,
in lap.

I have ten little
fingers,

I can shut them
up tight.

I can put them
all together,

Or make them
all hide.

. . . jump high . . .
. . . jump low . . .

And hold them all
just so.

Row, row, row your boat

Row, row, row your boat,
Gently down the stream,
Merrily, merrily, merrily, merrily,
Life is but a dream. *repeat*

Mime rowing action in rythm.

Row . . .   Row . . .   Row . . .   . . . your boat.

Peter works with one hammer

Peter works with one hammer, one hammer, one hammer,
Peter works with one hammer, this fine day.

Peter works with two hammers, *etc.*
Peter works with three hammers, *etc.*
Peter works with four hammers, *etc.*
Peter works with five hammers, *etc.*

Peter's very tired now, *etc.*
Peter's going to sleep now, *etc.*
Peter's waking up now, up now, up now,
Peter's waking up now this fine day.

ACTIONS

Verse 1 – One fist banging on knee in rhythm.
Verse 2 – Two fists banging on knees.
Verse 3 – Two fists banging. One foot tapping.
Verse 4 – Two fists banging. Two feet tapping.
Head nodding.

Bang fists on knees.
Peter works with two hammers,

Hands rub eyes and stretch out as if yawning.
Peter's very tired now,

Put head on hands, eyes closed.
Peter's going to sleep now . . .

Wake up and start hammering!
Peter's waking up now, up now . . . .

Little cottage

Little cottage in a wood,
Little man at a window stood,
Saw a rabbit running by,
Knocking at the door.
'Help me! help me! help me!' he cried,
'See the hunters on their way.'
'Little rabbit, come inside,
You'll be safe with me.'

Make roof of cottage with hands.

Look through hands for window.

Knock at door.

Shoot hands upward from shoulders and down while rabbit is talking.

'Point' for hunters, and beckon. Stroke hand (rabbit).

Little cottage in a wood,

Little man at the window stood,

. . . rabbit running by,

Knocking at the door.

'Help me! help me! help me!' he cried.

. . . come inside, . . .

You'll be safe with me.

Two fat gentlemen

Two fat gentlemen met in a lane,
Bowed most politely, bowed once again.
How do you do? How do you do?
How do you do again?

Two thin ladies met in a lane, *etc.*
Two tall policemen met in a lane, *etc.*
Two little schoolboys met in a lane, *etc.*
Two little babies met in a lane, *etc.*

Hold out fists with thumbs raised.

**Two fat gentlemen met
in a lane**

Bend each thumb slowly forward
in turn. Waggle each thumb in turn.

**Bowed most politely,
bowed once again.**

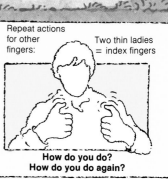

Repeat actions
for other
fingers:

Two thin ladies
= index fingers

**How do you do?
How do you do again?**

Here are Grandma's spectacles

Here are Grandma's spectacles,
And here is Grandma's hat,
And here's the way she folds her hands,
And puts them in her lap.

Here are Grandpa's spectacles,
And here is Grandpa's hat,
And here's the way he folds his arms,
And takes a little nap.

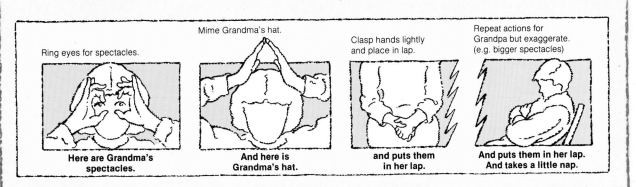

Ring eyes for spectacles.

Mime Grandma's hat.

Clasp hands lightly
and place in lap.

Repeat actions for
Grandpa but exaggerate.
(e.g. bigger spectacles)

**Here are Grandma's
spectacles.**

**And here is
Grandma's hat.**

**and puts them
in her lap.**

**And puts them in her lap.
And takes a little nap.**

23

Shoes

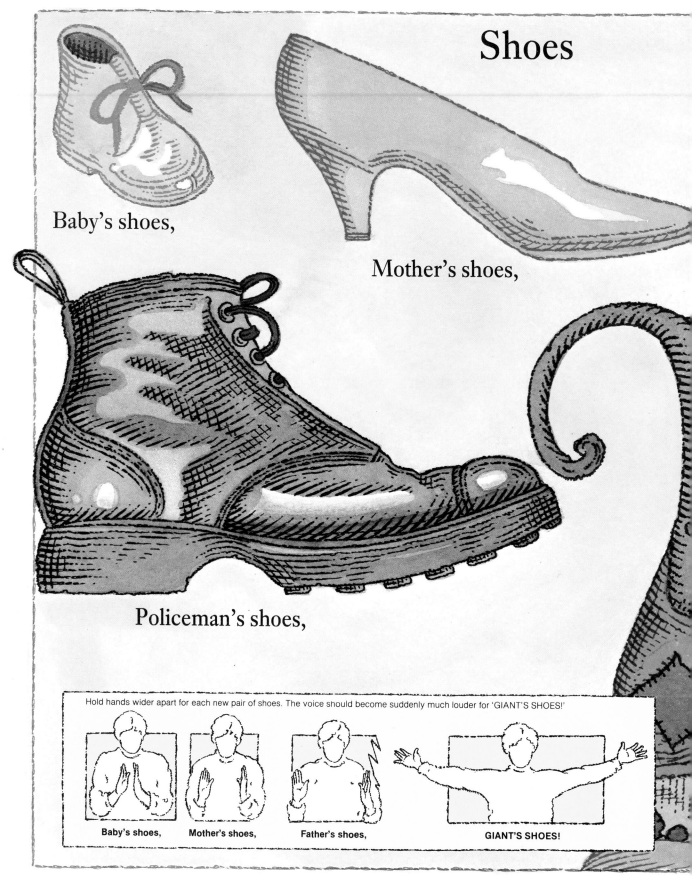

Baby's shoes,

Mother's shoes,

Policeman's shoes,

Hold hands wider apart for each new pair of shoes. The voice should become suddenly much louder for 'GIANT'S SHOES!'

Baby's shoes,   Mother's shoes,   Father's shoes,   GIANT'S SHOES!

Father's shoes,

GIANT'S SHOES!

Hickory, dickory, dock

Hickory, dickory, dock,
The mouse ran up the clock,

The clock struck ONE,
The mouse ran down,
Hickory, dickory, dock.

Run fingers lightly up arm.

Clap hands together.

Hickory, dickory, dock,

The mouse ran up the clock,

the clock struck ONE!

Hickory, Dickory, Dock.

My hands

My hands upon my head I place,

On my shoulders, on my face;
On my hips I place them – so,
Then bend down to touch my toe.
Now I raise them up so high,
Make my fingers fairly fly,
Now I clap them, one, two, three.
Then I fold them silently.

Place hands on top of head on shoulders and on cheeks.

Place hands on hips for 'so'. Bend down to touch toes.

Clap hands one, two, three and then Fold arms in rhythm.

My hands upon my head I place,

On my hips I place them — so.

Now I raise them up so high,

Now I clap them, one, two, three.

Then I fold them silently.

Cobbler, cobbler

Cobbler, cobbler, mend my shoe,
Get it done by half past two.
'Cos my toe is peeping through,
Cobbler, cobbler, mend my shoe.

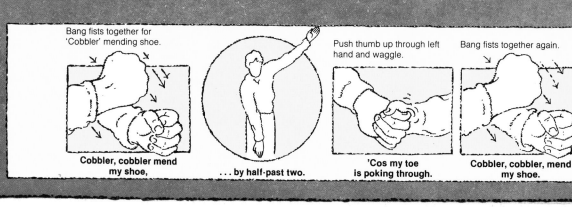

Bang fists together for 'Cobbler' mending shoe.

Cobbler, cobbler mend my shoe,

. . . by half-past two.

Push thumb up through left hand and waggle.

'Cos my toe is poking through.

Bang fists together again.

Cobbler, cobbler, mend my shoe.

Five fat peas

Five fat peas in a pea-pod pressed,
One grew, two grew and so did all the rest.
They grew, and they grew,
 and they grew, and they grew,
They grew so fat and portly that the
 pea-pod POPPED!

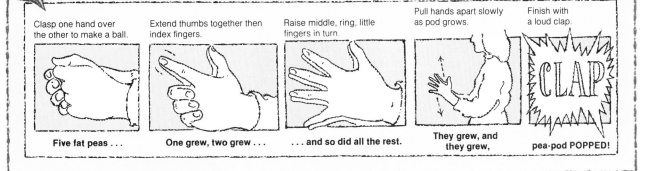

Clasp one hand over
the other to make a ball.

Extend thumbs together then
index fingers.

Raise middle, ring, little
fingers in turn.

Pull hands apart slowly
as pod grows.

Finish with
a loud clap.

Five fat peas . . .

One grew, two grew . . .

. . . and so did all the rest.

They grew, and
they grew,

pea-pod POPPED!

Knock at the door

Knock at the door,
Peep in,
Lift up the latch,
Walk in.
Chin Chopper, Chin Chopper,
Chin Chopper, CHIN!

Tap forehead in rhythm.	Point to eyes.	Tap end of nose in rhythm.	Open mouth, hold finger near.	Tap lightly under chin in rhythm. Finish with sudden tickle on last 'Chin'.
Knock-at-the-door	**Pee-p in**	**Lift-up-the-latch**	**Wa-lk in**	**. . . chin chopper, CHIN!**

Two little dicky birds

Two little dicky birds
Sitting on a wall.
One named Peter.
One named Paul.
Fly away Peter!
Fly away Paul!
Come back Peter.
Come back Paul.

Stick little piece of paper on each index finger.

Two little dicky birds sitting on a wall.

Hold out fists with index fingers raised. Shake each finger in turn (Peter, Paul).

One named Peter. One named Paul.

Toss each hand behind back. Bring back with middle fingers raised, index fingers hidden.

Fly away Peter! Fly away Paul!

Toss each hand behind back in turn again. Bring back index fingers raised, middle fingers tucked.

Come back Peter. Come back Paul.

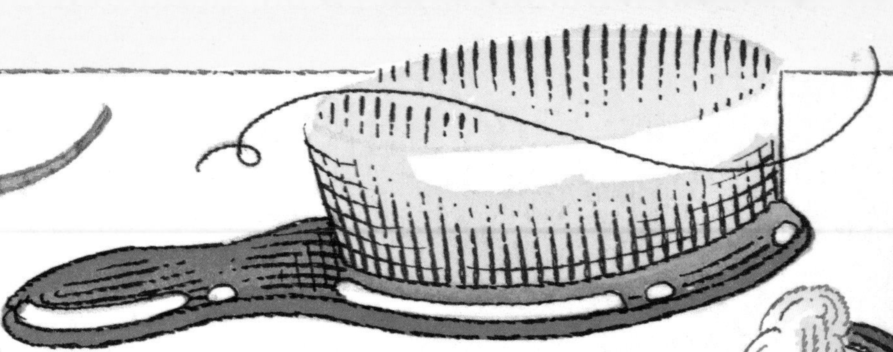

I can . . .

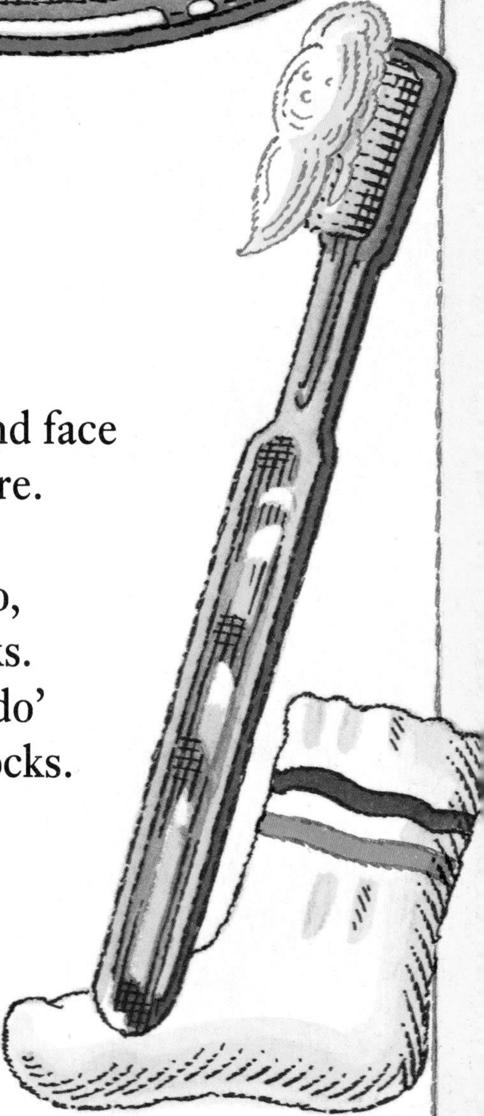

I can tie my shoe lace,
I can brush my hair,
I can wash my hands and face
And dry myself with care.

I can clean my teeth too,
And fasten up my frocks.
I can say 'How do you do'
And pull up both my socks.

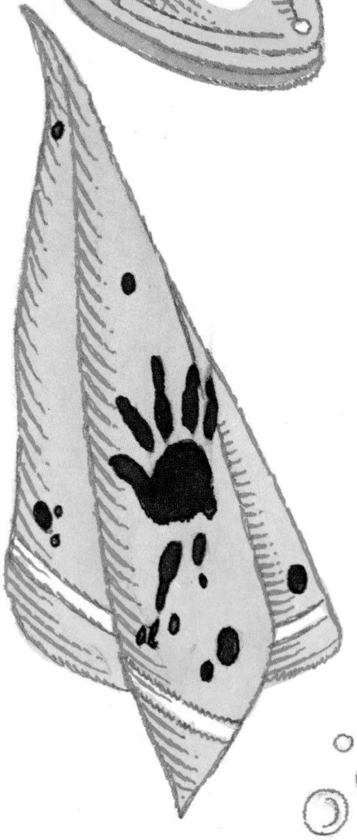

**(MIME ACTIONS IN RHYTHM
AND ON LAST LINE PUT HANDS IN LAP)**

Tall shop

Tall shop in the town.
Lifts moving up and down.
Doors swinging round about.
People moving in and out.

Move hands alternately.

Swing forearms open and shut.

Push fists backwards and forwards.

Tall shop in the town.

Lifts moving up and down.

Doors swinging round about.

People moving in and out.

The beehive

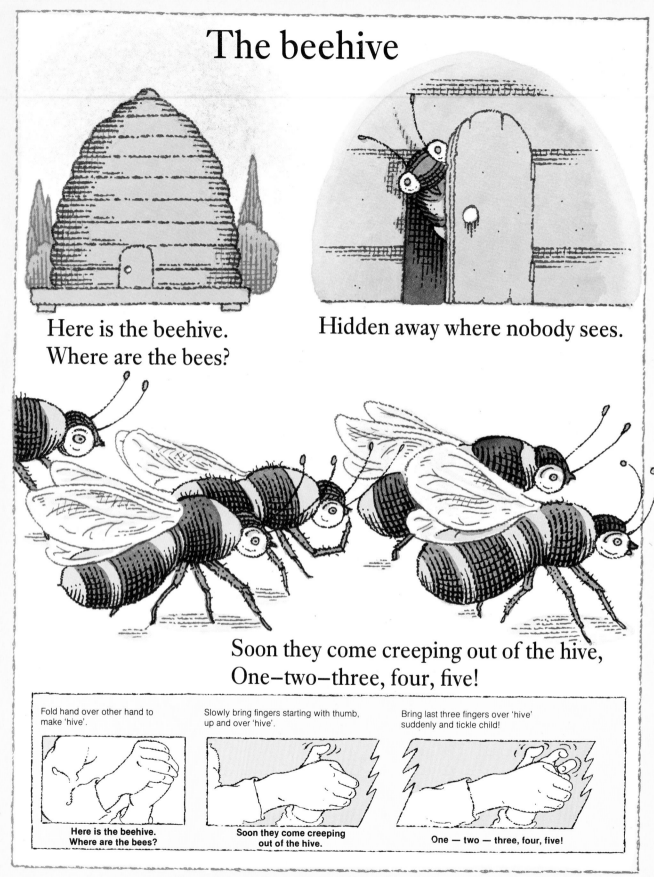

Here is the beehive.
Where are the bees?

Hidden away where nobody sees.

Soon they come creeping out of the hive,
One–two–three, four, five!

Fold hand over other hand to
make 'hive'.

Slowly bring fingers starting with thumb,
up and over 'hive'.

Bring last three fingers over 'hive'
suddenly and tickle child!

Here is the beehive.
Where are the bees?

Soon they come creeping
out of the hive.

One — two — three, four, five!

34

Tommy Thumb

Tommy Thumb, Tommy Thumb,
   where are you?
Here I am, here I am,
How do you do?

Peter Pointer, *etc.*
Middle Man, *etc.*
Ruby Ring, *etc.*
Baby Small, *etc.*

Fingers all, fingers all,
   where are you?
Here we are, here we are,
How do you do?

Make fists and hold them
out, extend thumbs and
wiggle them.

Tommy Thumb, Tommy Thumb,
Where are you?

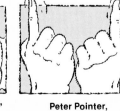

Continue through all the fingers as with the thumbs:
forefingers, middle fingers, ring fingers.

Peter Pointer,

Middle, Men etc.

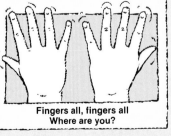

Make fists, extend all fingers and
then wiggle them.

Fingers all, fingers all
Where are you?

This little pig

This little pig went to market,
This little pig stayed at home;
This little pig had roast beef,
This little pig had none,
And this little pig cried,
'Wee-wee-wee-wee-wee',
All the way home.

Take child's big toe and give it a shake.

Shake each toe in turn.

Shake the smallest toe last.

Run fingers up child's leg and tickle fummy.

This little pig went to market

This little pig stayed at home;

This little pig had roast beef,

This little pig cried, 'Wee-wee-wee-wee-wee' all the way home.

I hear thunder

I hear thunder,
I hear thunder,
Oh! don't you?
Oh! don't you?
Pitter, patter raindrops.
Pitter, patter raindrops.
I'm wet through.
I'm wet through.

I see blue skies.
I see blue skies.
Way up high.
Way up high.
Hurry up the sunshine.
Hurry up the sunshine.
I'll soon dry.
I'll soon dry.

Hands behind ears pretend to listen and point to someone else.

Flutter hands down for rain, then pretend to be wet and finally point up to the sky.

Hands make circular motions in front of chest.

Sweep hands outwards and back.

I hear thunder ... Oh! don't you. | Pitter, patter raindrops. | I'm wet through. | Way up high. | Hurry up the sunshine. | I'll soon dry.

To the tune of Frère Jacques.

Pat-a-cake

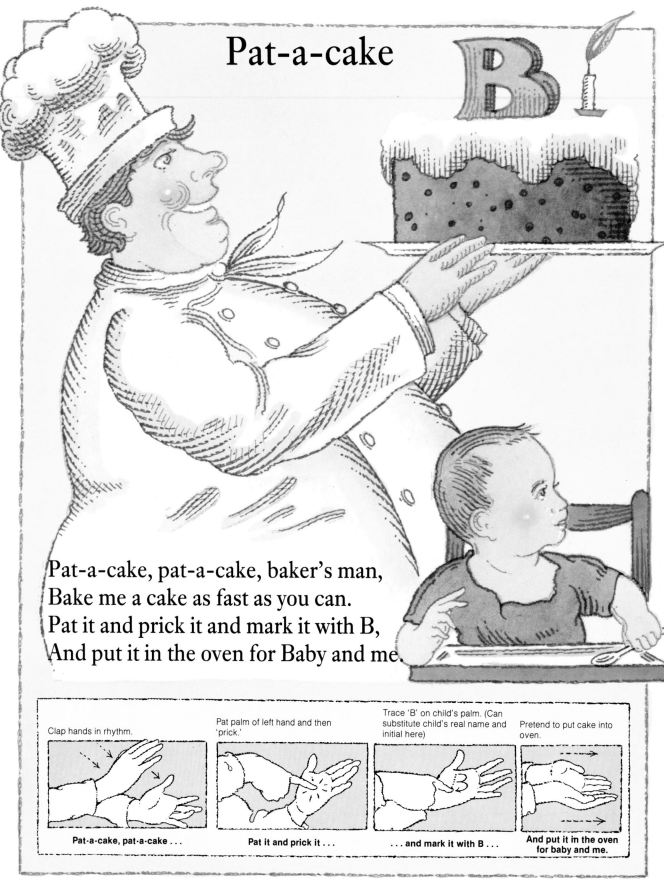

Pat-a-cake, pat-a-cake, baker's man,
Bake me a cake as fast as you can.
Pat it and prick it and mark it with B,
And put it in the oven for Baby and me.

Clap hands in rhythm.

Pat-a-cake, pat-a-cake . . .

Pat palm of left hand and then 'prick.'

Pat it and prick it . . .

Trace 'B' on child's palm. (Can substitute child's real name and initial here)

. . . and mark it with B . . .

Pretend to put cake into oven.

And put it in the oven for baby and me.

38

Here's a ball for baby

Here's a ball for baby,
Big and fat and round.
Here is baby's hammer,
See how it can pound.

Here are baby's soldiers,
Standing in a row.
Here is baby's music,
Clapping, clapping so.

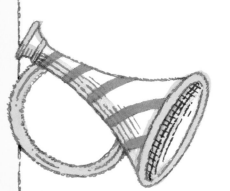

Here is baby's trumpet,
Tootle-tootle-oo.
Here's the way the baby
Plays at peek-a-boo.

Here's a big umbrella,
To keep the baby dry.
Here is baby's cradle,
Rock-a-baby-bye.

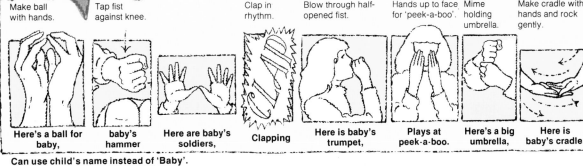

Make ball with hands.	Tap fist against knee.		Clap in rhythm.	Blow through half-opened fist.	Hands up to face for 'peek-a-boo'.	Mime holding umbrella.	Make cradle with hands and rock gently.
Here's a ball for baby,	baby's hammer	Here are baby's soldiers,	Clapping	Here is baby's trumpet,	Plays at peek-a-boo.	Here's a big umbrella,	Here is baby's cradle.

Can use child's name instead of 'Baby'.

Round about there

Round about there,
Sat a little hare,
A cat came and chased him,
Right up there!

Circle child's palm with finger.

Round about there,
Sat a little hare,

Walk finger slowly up arm.

A cat came and chased him,

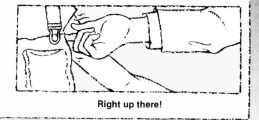

Tickle child suddenly under arm.

Right up there!

Here is the church

Here is the church,
And here's the steeple,
Open the doors,
And see all the people.

Here is the parson
Going upstairs,
And here's the parson
Saying his prayers.

Interlock fingers, for roof of church.

Raise index fingers for steeple.

Open thumbs showing 'congregation' of fingers.

Undo hands. Cross wrists and interlace fingers back to back in turn. Keeping fingers interlaced, drop hands down and up inside Hands facing out now, waggle thumb for 'Parson'.

Here is the church.

And here's the steeple.

Open the doors, And see all the people.

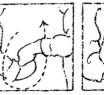

Here's the parson Going upstairs,

And here's the parson Saying his prayers.

Five little soldiers

Five little soldiers standing in a row,
Three stood straight,

And two stood – so.
Along came the captain,
And what do you think?
They ALL stood straight,
As quick as a wink.

Hold out hand
Five little soldiers

And two stood — so.

Pass index finger of other hand (Captain) in front.
Along came the captain,

And what do you think?

As index finger passes straighten fingers.
They ALL stood straight, As quick as a wink.

Here's the lady's knives and forks

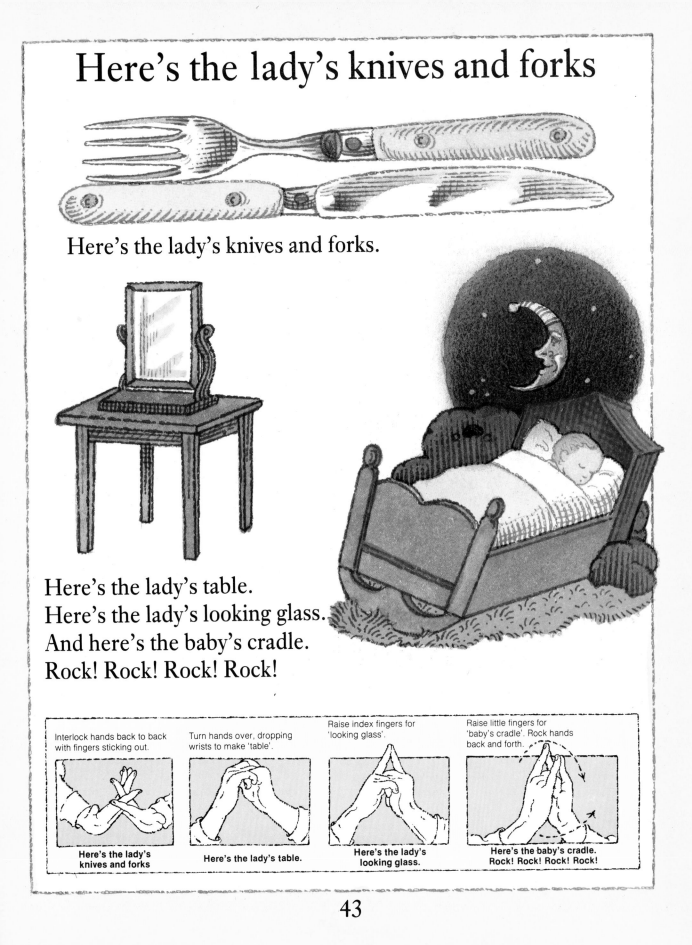

Here's the lady's knives and forks.

Here's the lady's table.
Here's the lady's looking glass.
And here's the baby's cradle.
Rock! Rock! Rock! Rock!

Interlock hands back to back with fingers sticking out.

Here's the lady's knives and forks

Turn hands over, dropping wrists to make 'table'.

Here's the lady's table.

Raise index fingers for 'looking glass'.

Here's the lady's looking glass.

Raise little fingers for 'baby's cradle'. Rock hands back and forth.

Here's the baby's cradle. Rock! Rock! Rock! Rock!

I'm a little teapot

I'm a little teapot, short and stout,
Here's my handle,
Here's my spout.
When I get the steam up, hear me shout,
'Tip me up and pour me out'.

Place hand on hip for handle.

Bend other arm and hand as 'spout'.

Bend over to one side to mime 'teapot' being poured.

Here's my handle

Here's my spout.

'Tip me up and pour me out'.

Clap your hands

Clap your hands, clap your hands,
Clap them just like me.

Touch your shoulders, touch your shoulders,
Touch them just like me.

Tap your knees, tap your knees,
Tap them just like me.

Shake your head, shake your head,
Shake it just like me.

Clap your hands, clap your hands,
Then let them quiet be.

ACTIONS.

Verse 1 — Clap hands in rhythm
Verse 2 — Touch shoulders
Verse 3 — Tap knees in rhythm
Verse 4 — Shake head in rhythm
Verse 5 — Clap hands and on last
             line put them in lap.

The cherry tree

Once I found a cherry stone,
I put it in the ground,
And when I came to look at it,
A tiny shoot I found.

The shoot grew up and up each day,
And soon became a tree.
I picked the rosy cherries then,
And ate them for my tea.

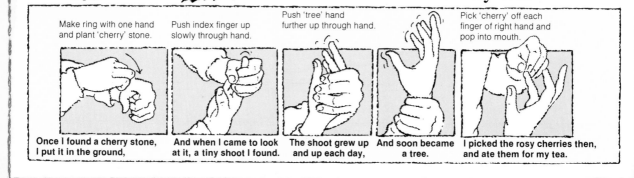

Make ring with one hand and plant 'cherry' stone.

Push index finger up slowly through hand.

Push 'tree' hand further up through hand.

Pick 'cherry' off each finger of right hand and pop into mouth.

Once I found a cherry stone, I put it in the ground,

And when I came to look at it, a tiny shoot I found.

The shoot grew up and up each day,

And soon became a tree.

I picked the rosy cherries then, and ate them for my tea.

The little bird

This little bird flaps its wings,
Flaps its wings, flaps its wings,
This little bird flaps its wings,
And flies away in the morning!

Flap outstretched fingers
like wings of a bird.

Lift hands still flapping as high as you can.

This little bird flaps its wings,

flaps its wings, flaps its wings,

This little birds flaps its wings,

And flies away in the morning!

For Sybil as well